THE HISTORY OF THE CONSTITUTION

A History Book for New Readers

— Written by —
Lisa Trusiani

— Illustrated by —
Isabella Grott

ROCKRIDGE PRESS

Dedicated to Grayson, Grant, Rick, Donna, Annamarie, Paul, Elaine, and Maria

Series Designer: Angela Navarra
Interior and Cover Designer: Jami Spittler
Art Producer: Tom Hood
Editor: Mary Colgan
Production Manager: Michael Kay
Production Editor: Melissa Edeburn

Paperback ISBN: 978-1-64876-372-4 | eBook ISBN: 978-1-64876-373-1
R0
Printed in China

CONTENTS

CHAPTER 1
SETTING THE STAGE

Understanding the Constitution

In 1787, the United States of America was a new nation with no president and no rules for electing one. The states—only 13 at the time—sent **delegates**, or representatives, to a meeting in Philadelphia, Pennsylvania, to determine how to select a leader and make laws for the nation. At the meeting, they created a brand-new government—and a constitution so powerful it changed the history of the world.

When the delegates voted for a leader to run the meeting, the winner was George Washington. He was a delegate from Virginia. Tall George took command of the meeting. His chair was higher than everyone else's. He listened more than he spoke. The delegates talked, argued, and made **compromises**, or agreements in which both sides give in a little. They wrote and rewrote the rules for their nation. After three months, the instructions for running the new nation were finished. They turned the United States of America into a **representative democracy**, where citizens vote for people to represent them in the government.

On September 17, 1787, the ink was dry, and the US Constitution was ready to be signed. It was four pages, each page the size of a poster. Thirty-nine delegates signed it. They believed it would help the new nation be strong and unified. The delegates, also called the Founders, designed the Constitution to be changed, or amended, over time. It has changed as the nation has changed. More than two hundred years later, the US Constitution is still the law of the land.

The Colonies Before the Constitution

The United States began as thirteen **colonies** owned and ruled by England. England allowed each colony to have its own government and make some laws. The people in the colonies, called colonists, voted for delegates to represent them in their colony's government. But they

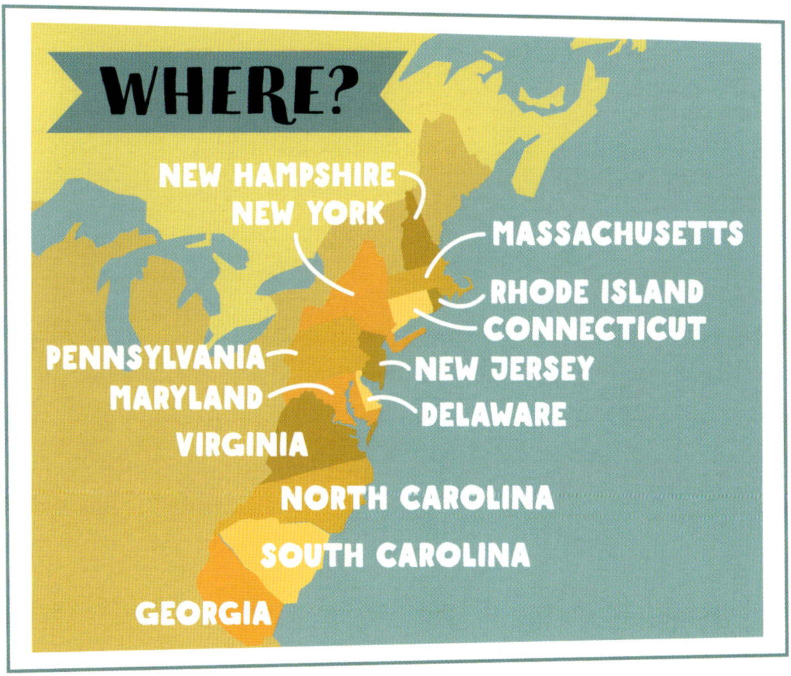

did not have any representatives in England's government, where many laws were made. Many of the colonists believed that these laws were not fair to them.

In 1776, leaders from the American colonies voted to break away from England. They wrote a document called the **Declaration of Independence**. It said the colonies were now states and part of a new nation, the United States of America, and England did not have the

right to rule them. The colonists sent the Declaration of Independence to England and got ready for war. They expected England would fight to stop them. They were right. England sent ships filled with soldiers to fight the Americans. The Revolutionary War had begun.

England's military was one of the greatest in the world. To defeat England, the American states needed to work together.

JUMP IN THE THINK TANK

Have you played a game with someone who had different rules? What happened? Did you follow their rules? Did they follow your rules? Did you create new rules together?

WHO?

George Washington (1732–1799) was a planter from Virginia. He led the United States of America to win the Revolutionary War against England and was elected its first president. He said, "The Constitution is the guide which I never will abandon."

They wrote the **Articles of Confederation**, instructions that created a **national** government to unite the states. After eight years of fighting, the United States of America won. It was a great victory. But the states had united only to fight a war. With the war over, the states went back to being independent. They did not know how to be a united country when they were not fighting a common enemy.

WHEN?

1776 — American colonies announce they are states and break away from England.

1777 — Articles of Confederation are written.

1781 — Articles of Confederation are ratified and go into effect.

CHAPTER 2

TROUBLE IN THE STATES

The Articles of Confederation

After the **Continental Congress** sent the Declaration of Independence to England, it needed to quickly form a legal government to prepare for England's attack. A national government would allow the states to join together to fight England. But what kind of national government could hold 13 independent states together? They did not want a strong

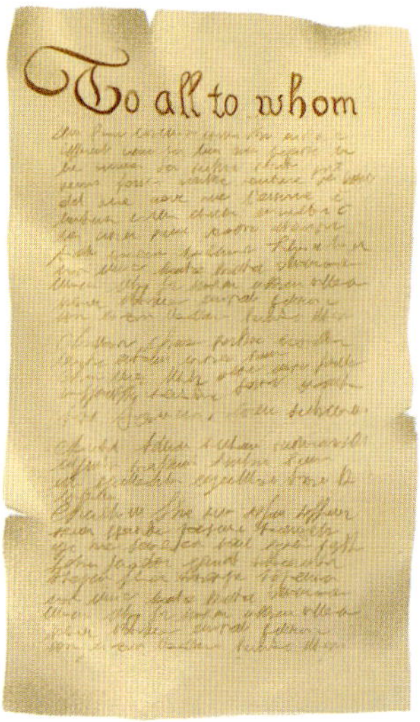

central government like England's. They wanted their states to be more powerful than any central government. They decided to form a weak national government that did not have the power to force states to obey laws.

The delegates wrote a document with instructions for running this government. It was called the Articles of Confederation. The Continental Congress would no longer exist. Instead, the Congress of the Confederation took its place. The national government could have an army and navy, send **ambassadors** to foreign nations to make deals, and declare war. But it could not charge **taxes** to pay for a war, or for anything else. It could borrow money and it did. The United States of America borrowed money from foreign countries to pay for the Revolutionary War. It also made a deal with France. France sent ships and soldiers to fight England, its old enemy. With help from France, the United States won the Revolutionary War.

After the war ended, the Articles of Confederation continued to allow the states to follow their own rules. Now they acted like separate countries. They were more independent than united. Leaders, including George Washington, worried the **union** would fall apart.

States vs. the Union

The Articles of Confederation allowed the states to be independent. They had their own armies, made their own deals with foreign countries, and printed their own money. They could also

charge taxes. People who didn't pay their taxes could be jailed. Or the state could take their farmland and other property and sell it. There were veterans (men who had been soldiers) who could not afford to pay taxes because they had not yet been paid for fighting in the Revolutionary War. Some people **protested** or rebelled. Some **rebellions** were violent.

JUMP -IN THE- THINK TANK

Have you ever felt that you were treated in an unfair way? What did you do when it happened? Were you able to talk to a parent or teacher about it?

Daniel Shays was a farmer and a veteran who helped lead a rebellion in Springfield, Massachusetts. Shays' Rebellion was an attack on the national arsenal where the federal government kept its weapons. Massachusetts paid for its own army to stop Shays' Rebellion. The Articles of Confederation did not allow the national government to charge taxes, so it did not have money to pay an army to stop rebellions, even to defend its own weapons.

The Articles of Confederation also caused problems when states tried to do business with each other. Delegates from five states went to a meeting, the Annapolis Convention. They wanted to make it easier for states to trade, or buy and sell, with each other. They all decided the Articles of Confederation had caused so many problems, it needed to be fixed. Alexander Hamilton, the delegate from New York, called on the Congress of the Confederation to set up a meeting with delegates from every state to fix the Articles of Confederation.

WHO?

Alexander Hamilton (1755 or 1757–1804) was born on an island in the Caribbean Sea. He immigrated to the American colonies to go to college. He became George Washington's assistant and helped the United States win the Revolutionary War. As secretary of the treasury under President George Washington, Alexander created the nation's banking system.

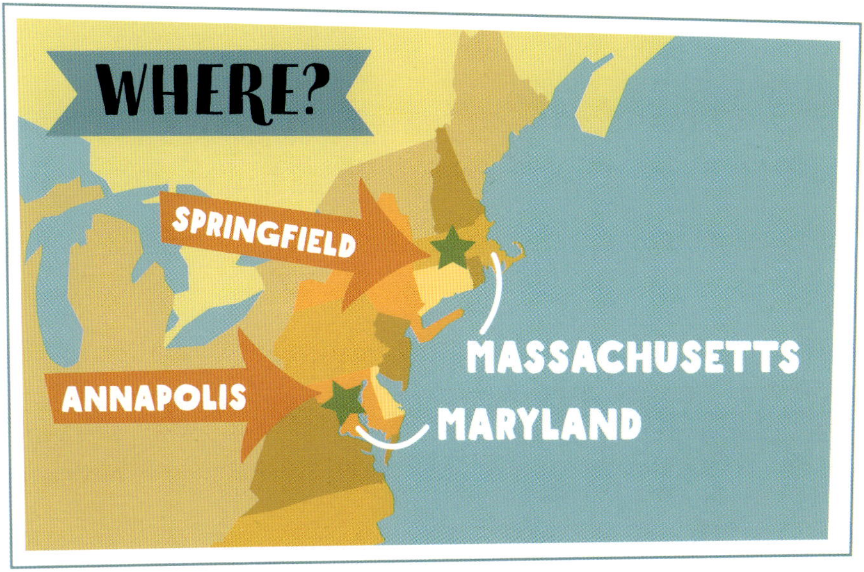

WHEN?

1783: The United States of America wins the Revolutionary War against England.

1786: The Annapolis Convention takes place in Annapolis, Maryland.

1787: Shays' Rebellion is stopped by the Massachusetts army.

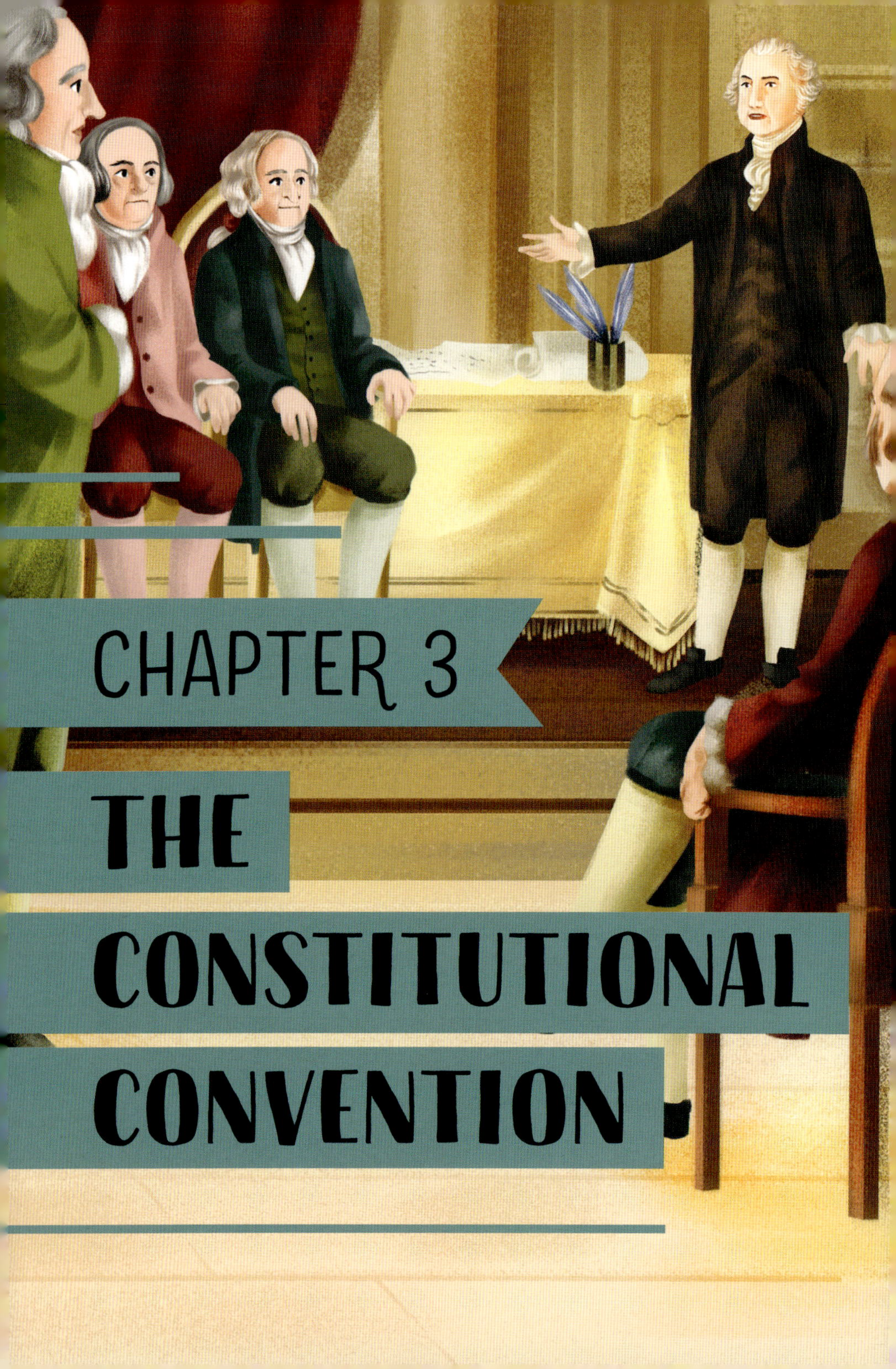

CHAPTER 3

THE CONSTITUTIONAL CONVENTION

A Special Invitation

It was May 1787 when states sent delegates to a meeting in Philadelphia, Pennsylvania, to fix the Articles of Confederation. It was called the Grand Convention. One state, Rhode Island, did not send anyone, but the other 12 states did. There were 55 delegates in total, and they were all white men. The delegates soon decided to toss out the Articles of Confederation and create a brand-new government. After three months, they had written the Constitution, instructions for their new nation. The name changed from the Grand Convention to the Constitutional Convention, the name used today.

Many of the delegates had served in the Revolutionary War. Most were merchants, planters, or lawyers. The youngest was 26 years old. Pennsylvania sent the oldest, the world-famous inventor Benjamin Franklin.

JUMP -IN THE- THINK TANK

Imagine that whenever your class votes on playing a game or watching a movie, the movie wins. Do you think it is fair never to play a game?

He was 81 years old, and he knew politics. Dr. Franklin had helped make deals between the United States and foreign countries. The state of Virginia sent seven delegates. Two would one day be presidents of the United States of America. George Washington, commander of the American military forces during the Revolutionary War, would be the nation's first president. James Madison would be the nation's fourth.

At this time, **slavery** was legal in the United States. Nearly half the delegates, including Benjamin Franklin, George Washington, and James Madison, owned or had owned enslaved persons. The delegates

argued about slavery. Southern states did not want the new national government to make slavery illegal. They believed an enslaved person was property, and people who owned property had rights. Other delegates disagreed. They believed slavery was wrong. They did not believe a person was property. For many years to come, the rest of the country would argue about slavery, too.

Let the Debates Begin!

In the 1700s, it was hard to travel a long way. Most people walked. The delegates did not. They went to Philadelphia by horse, horse and carriage, and boat. The first delegates to arrive, George Washington and James Madison, were from Virginia. Soon the other five delegates from Virginia joined them. Delegates from Philadelphia were already there. The meeting could not begin until most of the delegates

WHO?

Benjamin Franklin (1706–1790) was a printer, newspaper publisher, writer, landlord, scientist, inventor, and ambassador. He helped write the Declaration of Independence, the Treaty of Paris, and the Constitution.

from at least seven states had arrived. Bad weather had slowed them, and the convention began 11 days late. On May 25, 1787, there were enough delegates from enough states to begin the meeting. Right away they voted for George Washington to be the leader of the convention.

They also created rules for the meeting. One rule was secrecy. Whatever was said in the meeting was a secret. The delegates wanted to **debate** freely, and they did.

The debates were fiery. States with more people wanted to have more representatives in the national government. States with fewer people wanted every state to have the same number of representatives. There were also many arguments about slavery. Some delegates were **abolitionists**. They wanted the terrible system of enslaving people to end. Benjamin Franklin had owned several enslaved people in the past, but he

had freed them. At the time of the convention, he believed slavery was wrong. The state he represented, Pennsylvania, had passed a law in 1780 to put an end to slavery over time. Northern states would soon pass similar laws. Delegates from southern states held firm. If the Constitution could make slavery illegal someday, their states would break away from the union now.

WHEN?

There are enough delegates from enough states to open the Constitutional Convention (originally the Grand Convention).

MAY 25, 1787

Delegates debate how to select a president and how long a president should be in office.

JUNE 1, 1787

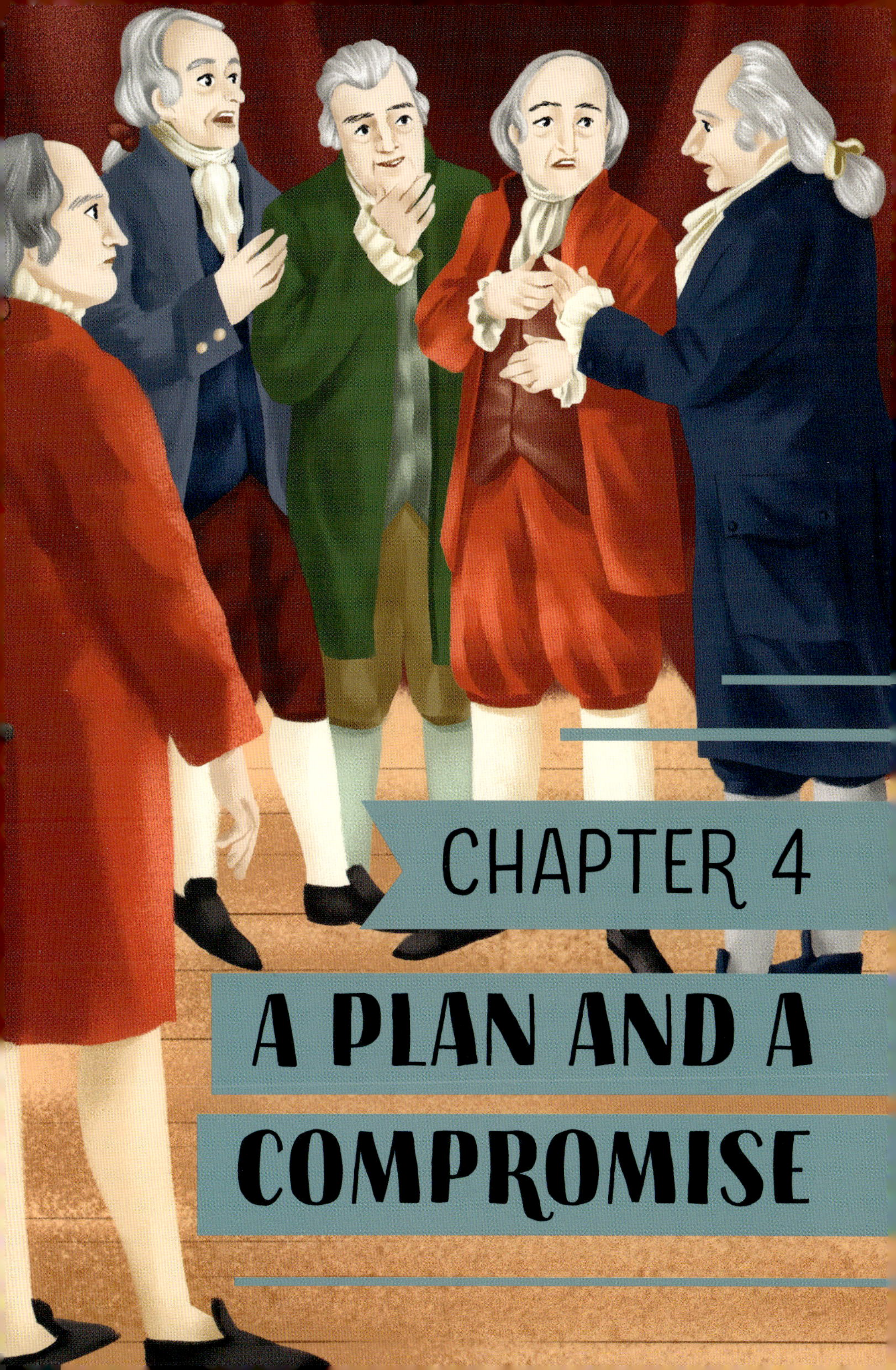

CHAPTER 4

A PLAN AND A COMPROMISE

James Madison and His Virginia Plan

The delegates decided the Articles of Confederation could not be fixed. But what would take its place? James Madison had

written a plan for running the new nation. Madison's Virginia Plan proposed a strong national government with three parts: Congress, the president, and the courts. Congress would be made up of a lower house of lawmakers and an upper house of lawmakers. Today the United States has the same three parts: Congress makes the laws, the president enforces the laws, and the courts explain the laws.

> The Constitution . . . was not, like the fabled Goddess of Wisdom, the offspring of a single brain. It ought to be regarded as the work of many heads and many hands.
>
> *—James Madison*

The Virginia Plan would make the national government larger and more powerful. Some delegates liked this. Others did not. Large states liked the Virginia Plan's **proportional representation** which would base the number of delegates on a state's population, so large states would have more delegates because they had more people. Another plan, the New Jersey Plan, proposed **equal representation**, whereby small and large states would have the same number of delegates. Small states liked this plan. But the New Jersey Plan was so much like the Articles of Confederation, no one voted for it.

Over time, the delegates took Madison's Virginia Plan and added a system of **checks and balances**. Congress, the president, and the courts would be separate, and they would have equal power. One part could check, or stop, another from taking too much power. It is the system used today in the United States.

Controversial Compromise

Massachusetts, Pennsylvania, and Virginia were large states with hundreds of thousands of people. Delaware, New Hampshire, and New Jersey were small states with tens of thousands. Large states and small states could not agree on how many delegates each state would send to Congress. The Constitutional Convention closed to celebrate **Independence Day**. Would any of the delegates change his mind during the **recess**? When they returned, Roger Sherman, a delegate from Connecticut, proposed a compromise. The number of lawmakers would be different for the two houses in Congress. In the lower house, today's **House of Representatives**, the number of delegates would be based on a state's population; large states would have more delegates than small states. In the upper house, today's **Senate**, each state would have the same number. Large and small states both liked Sherman's Great Compromise.

WHO?

Roger Sherman (1721–1793) learned shoemaking from his father. He went to school but learned best by reading as much as possible. He read so much and learned so well that he passed the exam to become a lawyer. He worked as a merchant, a judge, and a lawmaker. He had 15 children.

JUMP -IN THE- THINK TANK

A compromise happens when two people who disagree each give up some of what they want and meet in the middle. Do you think compromise is always good?

Southern states and northern states had debates about counting people—and *which* people counted. The South had farms as big as towns where enslaved people worked for no pay. For every ten persons living in the South, four were enslaved. The North had many small farms, fishing boats, and industry. They had fewer enslaved people. Southern states wanted to count all enslaved people so they would have more delegates in Congress. Northern states wanted only free people to count. They did not want the South to get more political power because of slavery, a system that was terrible and wrong. North and South each gave up some of what they wanted to agree on a compromise. The Three-Fifths Compromise allowed each state to add 60 percent, or three-fifths, of the number of enslaved people to the number of free people. Free people were counted the same whether black or white. Many delegates believed the Three-Fifths Compromise was a terrible price to pay to keep the states united.

WHEN?

Debate continues over representation in Congress.

JUNE 29–30, 1787

The Great Compromise passes by one vote in the convention.

JULY 16, 1787

CHAPTER 5

FILLING IN THE DETAILS

The Executive Branch

Executive means leader, and the **executive branch** is the part of government with the president. But what did "president" mean to the delegates? One delegate wanted three people to be president. Another wanted one person to be president for life. They were interesting ideas, but the delegates decided the president would be one person elected for four years. Also, a president must have been born in the United States, have lived there for at least 14 years, and be 35 years old or older.

The delegates had many questions. Who would elect the president, Congress or the citizens? If it was Congress, wouldn't that make Congress more powerful than the president? If citizens elected the president, did they know enough to elect a good one? Delegates agreed that citizens could elect good lawmakers to represent their states in the national Congress, because citizens knew their states well. But did they know enough to elect a good president? The delegates debated and voted more than 60 times. They went to local taverns to share meals while they continued to argue and discuss. They could not agree.

Again, there was a compromise. The delegates created **electors**, people who represent the citizens of a state during a presidential election. Electors are like super-voters and each state has some. A state has as many electors as it has

lawmakers in Congress. Every four years, there is a presidential election. Citizens vote in their states, their votes are counted, and the candidate with the most votes wins the state. Electors then vote for their state's winner. Today there are 538 electors, and each has one vote. A candidate must get more than half of all electoral votes (270 votes or more) to win and become president.

The Judicial Branch

Courts and judges are the **judicial branch** of the government. People go to court to settle a dispute, or disagreement. Both sides bring

WHO?

James Wilson (1742–1798) was born in Scotland, moved to the colonies, and became a lawyer. He represented Pennsylvania at the Constitutional Convention. Many of his ideas are in the Constitution.

lawyers to tell the judge why they should win. Judges have studied the law. After listening to both sides, the judge applies the law. This means judges use the law to decide which side wins the dispute. The side that does not win can go to a "higher" court and try again. The highest court in the United States is the Supreme Court.

> Far from being above the laws, [the president] is amenable to them in his private character as a citizen, and in his public character by impeachment.
>
> *—James Wilson*

At the convention, delegates wanted to create a judicial branch as powerful as the president and Congress. It had to be independent, too. Would Supreme Court justices be independent if they were elected every four years?

Delegates worried they might not use the law to decide which side wins a dispute. They might give the win to people who could help them get elected. The delegates decided that Supreme Court justices would work for as long as they were able. When it was time to hire a new judge, the president would choose a justice, but Congress would decide whether the justice was hired.

Supreme Court justices use the Constitution to decide which side wins. In 1875, a woman went to the Supreme Court to say she had the right to vote. The Supreme Court decided she did not. Right away people worked to change the Constitution. Women protested over many years. It took 45 years, but in 1920, the 19th Amendment was added. It promised women the right to vote.

JUMP —IN THE— THINK TANK

If you were president of your class, would you want to be the only president, or would you want two other students to be president with you? Why?

However, only white women could vote starting in 1920. It took another 45 years, but the Voting Rights Act became law in 1965, making it illegal to stop any person from voting.

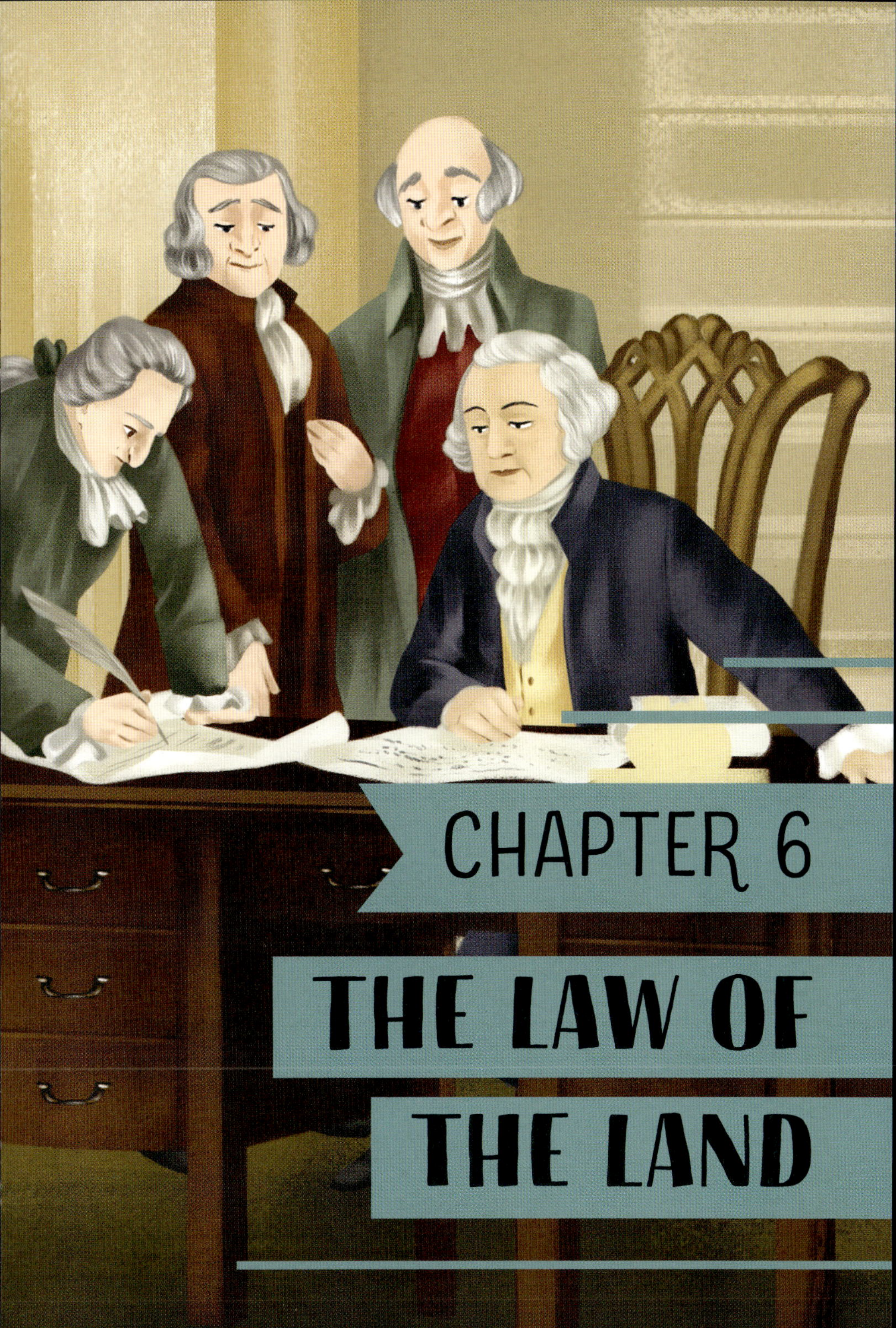

CHAPTER 6
THE LAW OF THE LAND

The Legislative Branch

Congress is the **legislative branch**, the part of the government that makes laws for the nation. Delegates spent weeks debating how many lawmakers each state would send to the new national Congress, and who would elect them. Finally, the delegates decided. There would be two groups of lawmakers, the House of Representatives and the Senate. Large states could send more people to the House of Representatives because the number would be based on a state's population, which is the number of people living there. Representatives would be

WHO?

Gouverneur Morris (1752–1816) was born in New York. At 19 years old, he passed the exam to become a lawyer. Morris wrote the final draft of the Constitution at the convention.

elected by the people directly, and they would work for two years. The Senate was different. No matter how large or small the state was, it would have the same number of lawmakers, or senators. They would be elected by a state's lawmakers and work for six years. For more than 100 years, the House and Senate worked like this. In 1913, the Constitution was changed to have people elect their senators directly.

> "The people are the king."
> — ***Gouverneur Morris***

Since its early days, Congress has made thousands of national laws. How is a law made? Most often a law is a bill first. A legislative bill is a document that explains how the law would work. Anyone elected to the House of Representatives or to the Senate can write a bill. A bill becomes law when most representatives in the House of Representatives and most senators in the Senate vote for it, and the president signs it. A law can be as simple as naming a park. It can be as important as stopping polluters or protecting animals from becoming extinct. Congress meets in the Capitol building, which was built in 1846.

Signed, Sealed, Delivered

By the end of July, the delegates had agreed on many rules for running their new government. Five delegates were chosen to be on the Committee of Detail and write the first draft of the Constitution. On August 6, they gave copies

to all the delegates, who debated and made more changes. A new group of delegates, including Gouverneur Morris from Pennsylvania, formed the Committee of Style to write the next draft of the Constitution. Back then most citizens felt closer to their state than their country. Morris wanted to remind citizens that before they were New Yorkers or Virginians, they were Americans. He changed the beginning of the Constitution from, "We the people of the states of New Hampshire, Massachusetts," etc., to "We the people of the United States."

JUMP —IN THE— THINK TANK

Listening to other people is important during a debate. Do you think people who are debating with each other sometimes change their minds? Why do you think it was important for the delegates to debate the Constitution?

On September 17, 1787, the Constitution was ready to be signed. One by one, 38 delegates dipped a **quill pen** into ink and wrote their names at the bottom of the document. It was time to celebrate.

They had written the Constitution. But there was more work to be done. The Constitution would not replace the Articles of the Confederation until 9 of the 13 states had **ratified**, or approved, it. The Confederation Congress sent the Constitution to all 13 states. People voted for delegates to go to state conventions to vote for or against the Constitution. The Constitution and its new government were debated in the newspapers, at special meetings, and anywhere Americans stopped to chat. On June 21, 1788, New Hampshire became the ninth state to ratify it, and the Constitution officially became the law of the land.

WHEN?

The Committee of Detail is formed to write first draft of the Constitution.

JULY 24, 1787

Debate begins after the Committee of Detail presents first draft of the Constitution.

AUGUST 6, 1787

The Committee of Style is formed to add approved changes to the Constitution.

SEPTEMBER 8, 1787

The Committee of Style presents a final draft of the Constitution to be voted on.

SEPTEMBER 12, 1787

Delegates vote to adopt the Constitution.

SEPTEMBER 15, 1787

Thirty-eight delegates sign the Constitution. It does not yet have a Bill of Rights.

SEPTEMBER 17, 1787

The Constitution is published for everyone to read.

SEPTEMBER 19, 1787

The Constitution is ratified by the ninth state.

JUNE 21, 1788

The US Congress under the Constitution opens.

MARCH 4, 1789

CHAPTER 7

BUILDING THE NATION

We Have Rights

After the Constitutional Convention, Americans had read the Constitution and were not satisfied. They had expected to see their freedoms and rights written into the Constitution, but they weren't there. There were several reasons. Freedoms and rights were in the states' constitutions, and some delegates to the convention believed this was good enough. They did not want to spend months debating each and every right and delay getting the national Constitution ratified.

Delegates went back to their states and explained that after the Constitution was ratified, it could be changed. Freedoms and rights could be added. States had meetings to approve or reject the Constitution. Nine of the 13 states approved. This was enough to ratify the Constitution, and it became the law of the land. Next they formed the new national government. Each state chose their electors, people who would vote for the president and vice president. When the electors voted, it was **unanimous**. George Washington received every vote and became the country's first president. As many as 10,000 people came to watch his inauguration. John Adams won the most votes for vice president. States held elections for people to represent them in the national House of Representatives and Senate. The new government was in place.

Now it was time to work on the Constitution again. James Madison wrote amendments that

WHO?

James Madison (1751–1836) was born in Virginia and went to Princeton University before it had that name. He is called the Father of the Constitution because so many of his words and ideas are in the Constitution.

describe Americans' rights. These amendments are called the Bill of Rights. The national House of Representatives and Senate made changes and approved 10 amendments. The Bill of Rights was sent to all the states to be debated and approved. On December 15, 1791, the Bill of Rights was ratified and became the first 10 amendments to the Constitution. These rights include freedom of speech and the right to a fair trial.

Today's Constitution

The Constitution is now more than 200 years old. It is stronger today than it was when it was first written. Very smartly, the men who wrote the Constitution included instructions for changing it. It is not easy to change it, but it can be done, and it has been done. The first change was in 1791 when the 10 amendments that make up the Bill of Rights were added. At the beginning, the Constitution and the Bill of Rights did not protect all Americans equally. White men who owned land had more rights. Over time, the nation changed, and Americans changed the Constitution. Instead of 10 amendments, there

> “In a word, as a man is said to have a right to his property, he may be equally said to have a property in his rights. Where an excess of power prevails, property of no sort is duly respected. No man is safe in his opinions, his person, his faculties, or his possessions.”
>
> — ***James Madison***

are now 27. Today the Constitution protects all citizens, not only white men with property.

Eight months after the end of the Civil War, the 13th Amendment was ratified. It made slavery illegal. Three years later, the 14th Amendment was ratified to protect the rights of people who had been enslaved. It promised all citizens "equal protection of the laws." This "equal protection" has continued to protect the rights of Americans to this day. Over the years, the Supreme Court used the 14th Amendment to decide it is legal for people of different races to marry each other and for men to marry men and women to marry women.

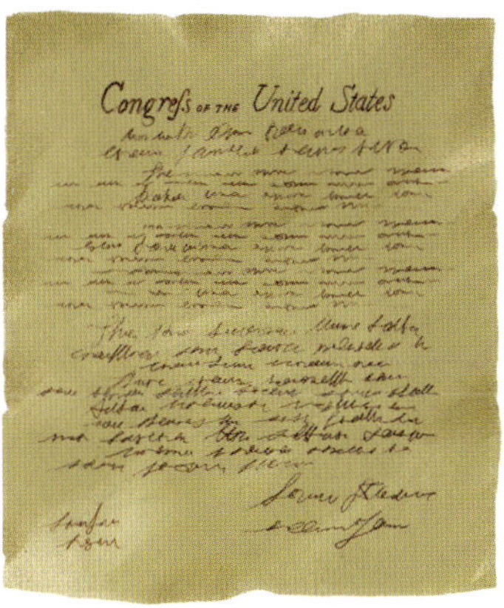

JUMP –IN THE– THINK TANK

What do you think it means when someone says, "I do not agree with what you say, but I defend your right to say it?"

The men who wrote the Constitution did not drive cars, talk on phones, or use computers. Yet they created a constitution that is still used today, and it has lasted longer than any other written constitution in the modern world.

WHEN?

1791 — The Bill of Rights is ratified by enough states and becomes part of the Constitution.

1865 — The 13th Amendment abolishes slavery.

1868 — The 14th Amendment provides all citizens with equal protection under the laws.

1967 — The Supreme Court decides people of any race have a legal right to marry each other.

2015 — The Supreme Court decides people of the same sex, or gender, have a legal right to marry each other.

CHAPTER 8

SO . . . WHAT'S THE STORY OF THE CONSTITUTION ?

Challenge Accepted!

The Constitution is a legal document that explains how the United States must be run. It has the basic laws, instructions, and rules for the country.

Let's test your knowledge of the Constitution in a who, what, when, where, why, and how quiz. Feel free to look back in the text to find the answers, but try to remember them first.

1 Where was the Constitutional Convention held?

- A Savannah, Georgia
- B Brooklyn, New York
- C Philadelphia, Pennsylvania
- D Boston, Massachusetts

2 Who did the delegates vote to be the leader of the convention?

- A Alexander Hamilton
- B Benjamin Franklin
- C Gouverneur Morris
- D George Washington

3 **Who was James Madison?**

- A Virginia delegate to the Constitutional Convention
- B Author of the Bill of Rights
- C Fourth president of the United States
- D All of the above

4 **Who was 81 years old and the oldest delegate to the Constitutional Convention?**

- A George Washington
- B James Wilson
- C Alexander Hamilton
- D Benjamin Franklin

5 **The president is in what part of the government?**

- A Legislative branch
- B Judicial branch
- C Executive branch
- D All of the above

6 **Courtsandjudgesareinwhatpartof the government?**

- A Legislative branch
- B Judicial branch
- C Executive branch
- D All of the above

7 **The House of Representatives and the Senate are in what part of the government?**

- A Legislative branch
- B Judicial branch
- C Executive branch
- D All of the above

8 **Why are checks and balances in the Constitution?**

- A To stop any one branch of the government from becoming too powerful
- B To help the executive branch become the most powerful
- C To help the legislative branch become the most powerful
- D To help the judicial branch become the most powerful

9 **What did the Constitution replace?**

- A Treaty of Paris
- B Magna Carta
- C Articles of Confederation
- D Declaration of Independence

10 **What are the first three words of the Constitution?**

- A We the Brave
- B We the People
- C We the Americans
- D We the Champions

Answers: 1. C; 2. D; 3. D; 4. D; 5. C; 6. B; 7. A; 8. A; 9. C; 10. B

Our World

Life in the United States was very different hundreds of years ago when the Constitution was written. Yet today the Constitution is still the highest law of the land. Let's look at some ways the Constitution protects Americans.

→ Is there a church, a mosque, or a synagogue in your town? Do you know people who believe there is no God? The Constitution protects a person's right to practice any religion or to have no religion at all.

→ More women are professional firefighters and more men are nurses than ever before. The Constitution does not allow employers to discriminate against people because of gender.

→ Sometimes adults try to ban a book and remove it from a library. The Supreme Court used the Constitution to decide that public schools cannot ban and remove a book just because they don't like the ideas in it.

JUMP IN THE THINK TANK FOR MORE!

The Constitution is called a living document because it can be changed. Since the time it was ratified more than 200 years ago, 27 amendments have been added. These amendments explain the rights and freedoms that Americans have.

→ Think about freedom of speech, freedom of the press, freedom of assembly (meeting), freedom to practice any religion or none, and the right to vote. Do you think one is more important than another? Why?

→ Do you think it's important for Americans to know what rights and freedoms are protected by the Constitution? Do you think children should have the same rights as adults?

→ Would you rather live in a country with a powerful king or in a country with a powerful constitution that allows people to rule themselves and protects their rights and freedoms? Why?

Glossary

abolitionist: A person who wanted slavery to be outlawed, or made illegal

ambassadors: Official representatives sent by one nation to another nation

Articles of Confederation: An agreement between the original 13 US states describing the details of their partnership

checks and balances: Creating separate branches of government—executive, legislative, and judicial—and giving each branch ways to keep the other two branches from taking too much power

colony: Land owned by a country, usually a country that is far away. More than one colony is colonies; people who live there are colonists.

compromise: An agreement that is made when both sides give in a little (or a lot)

Continental Congress: A group of delegates from the original 13 colonies

debate: To argue about a specific topic

Declaration of Independence: The 1776 document announcing the American colonies were a separate country and no longer part of England

delegate: A person chosen to act for or represent others

electors: People who represent the citizens of a state during a presidential election and vote for their state's winner

equal representation: Every state having the same number of representatives

executive branch: The branch of government responsible for carrying out laws

House of Representatives: A group of lawmakers, each elected by citizens of their state to work for two years, who meet to make laws for the United States

Independence Day: Another way to say "Fourth of July," a national holiday in the United States first celebrated on July 4, 1776, when the Second Continental Congress signed the Declaration of Independence and broke away from England

judicial branch: The part of government that has courts and judges

legislative branch: The part of government that has elected officials creating laws

national: Having to do with the whole country or nation

proportional representation: When the number of representatives is based on the number of people living in a state

protest: To publicly show you disagree with something

quill pen: A pen made from the feather of a large bird

ratify: To approve in a formal way

rebellion: The act of going against an authority

recess: A formal break, interruption, or time off

representative democracy: A government made up of people who have been elected to make laws and act for its citizens

Senate: A group of lawmakers, each elected by citizens of their state to work for six years, who meet to make laws for the United States

slavery: A system in which people are treated like property and forced to work against their will for no pay

taxes: Money the government collects from its citizens to help pay for things everyone needs, like schools and roads

unanimous: Total agreement between two or more people

union: Another way to say the United States of America

Bibliography

Garner, Tom. "The US Constitution: Facts about the Country's Founding Document." *All About History*. July 3, 2020. LiveScience.com/US-Constitution.html.

George Washington's Mount Vernon. "Teaching the Constitution." n.d. MountVernon.org/education/for-teachers/digital-resources-for-your-classroom/teaching-the-constitution.

Hakim, Joy. *A History of US: From Colonies to Country: 1735–1791*, Third Revised Edition. New York: Oxford University Press, 2007.

James Madison University. "About James Madison." n.d. JMU.edu/civic/madison.shtml.

Kelly, Martin. "Why the Articles of Confederation Failed." ThoughtCo.com. Last updated May 8, 2020. Accessed October 2, 2020. ThoughtCo.com/why-articles-of-confederation-failed-104674.

Longley, Robert. "Continental Congress: History, Significance, and Purpose." ThoughtCo.com. Last updated September 8, 2020. Accessed October 30, 2020. ThoughtCo.com/continental-congress-5074199.

Longley, Robert. "Shays' Rebellion of 1786." ThoughtCo.com. Last updated June 2, 2020. Accessed August 28, 2020. ThoughtCo.com/shays-rebellion-causes-effects-4158282.

Mass Humanities. "Rebels Attack Springfield Arsenal." *Mass Moments* (blog). n.d. MassMoments.org/moment-details/rebels-attack-springfield-arsenal.html.

Mosvick, Nicholas. "On This Day, Supreme Court Refuses Women Right to Vote." *Constitution Daily* (blog). March 29, 2020. ConstitutionCenter.org/blog/on-this-day-supreme-court-refuses-women-right-to-vote.

Rossiter, Clinton. *1787: The Grand Convention*. New York: The Macmillan Company, 1966.

Supreme Court of the United States. "The Supreme Court at Work." n.d. SupremeCourt.gov/about/courtatwork.aspx.

Treanor, William. *SCOTUSblog.com*. August 5, 2019. SCOTUSblog.com/2019/08/the-framers-intent-gouverneur-morris-the-committee-of-style-and-the-creation-of-the-federalist-constitution.

US National Archives and Records Administration. "Founders Online." Founders.Archives.gov.

About the Author

LISA TRUSIANI has written hundreds of comics stories and nonfiction books for children. Her work has received the iParenting Media HOT Award, National Parenting Center Award, NAPPA Parenting Publishing GOLD Award, several Parents' Choice Awards, and the Lupine Honors Award from the Maine Library Association. She is happiest writing for children and spending time with her family and friends. Lisa feels completely at home in her birthplace, the great state of Maine; her father's ancestral village, San Polo dei Cavalieri, Italy; and her heart space, Maplewood, New Jersey.

About the Illustrator

ISABELLA GROTT was born in 1985 in Rovereto, a small town in northern Italy. As a child, she loved to draw and play outside with Perla, her beautiful German Shepherd. She studied at Nemo Academy of Digital Arts in the city of Florence, where she currently lives with her cat, Miss Marple. She works digitally but also with traditional tools, such as pencils, watercolors, and crayons. Isabella loves traveling, watching movies, and reading—a lot! In fact, if she hadn't become an illustrator, today she would certainly be a librarian!